THE DREAM BUILDER'S BLUEPRINT

DR. KING'S MESSAGE TO YOUNG PEOPLE

Alice Faye Duncan

Illustrated by

E. B. Lewis

CALKINS CREEK
AN IMPRINT OF
ASTRA BOOKS FOR YOUNG READERS
New York

THE DREAM BUILDER'S BLUEPRINT

Dr. Martin Luther King Jr. seldom spoke in elementary or middle school auditoriums during his travels as a civil rights leader and Nobel Peace Prize winner. Usually, he stood in church pulpits and spoke at large freedom rallies filled with college students and adults. Six months before his assassination in Memphis, Dr. King cleared his schedule to visit the seventh-to-ninth-grade students at Barratt Junior High in South Philadelphia. The date was Thursday, October 26, 1967. While the event is unknown to most, Dr. King's Barratt visit is important because on this rare occasion, he shaped his words specifically for school-age children. As college activists in the 1960s became more militant in their beliefs, Dr. King pursued social change using forms of nonviolent protests. He reminded Barratt students that violence does not promote progress.

I composed an erasure poem to offer a contemporary interpretation of Dr. King's Barratt speech, "What Is Your Life's Blueprint?" Erasure poems are a type of *found poetry*. That term means that the words come from a longer source like a newspaper article, a novel, or a speech. Text in an erasure poem is selected from the sequence of words as they appear in the longer document. Erasure poems work with the original source to amplify the meaning or work against the original source to emphasize a contradiction. Some erasure poems are also composed for the joy of complete nonsense.

I erased 1,488 words from Dr. King's speech of 1,765 words. During my creative process, I discovered that the gift of poetry is its ability to share big ideas with few words. In the poetic equation, less is more. With the 277 words that remain, I offer readers a new creation titled "The Dream Builder's Blueprint." My erasure poem amplifies Dr. King's message of nonviolence, to remind readers that a rewarding blueprint for life requires one to:

PLAN
CELEBRATE SELF
PRACTICE
EXCELLENCE
SEEK JUSTICE
KEEP MOVING

A blueprint serves as the pattern for those building a building.

I want to suggest things that should be in your life's blueprint.

NUMBER ONE . . .

You count.
You have worth.

FEEL THAT.

Say, "I am Black . . .
Beautiful . . .
Good."

BELIEVE THAT.

SECONDLY—ACHIEVE EXCELLENCE.

As years unfold, young friends,
doors of opportunity are opening.
The challenge is to be ready as they open.

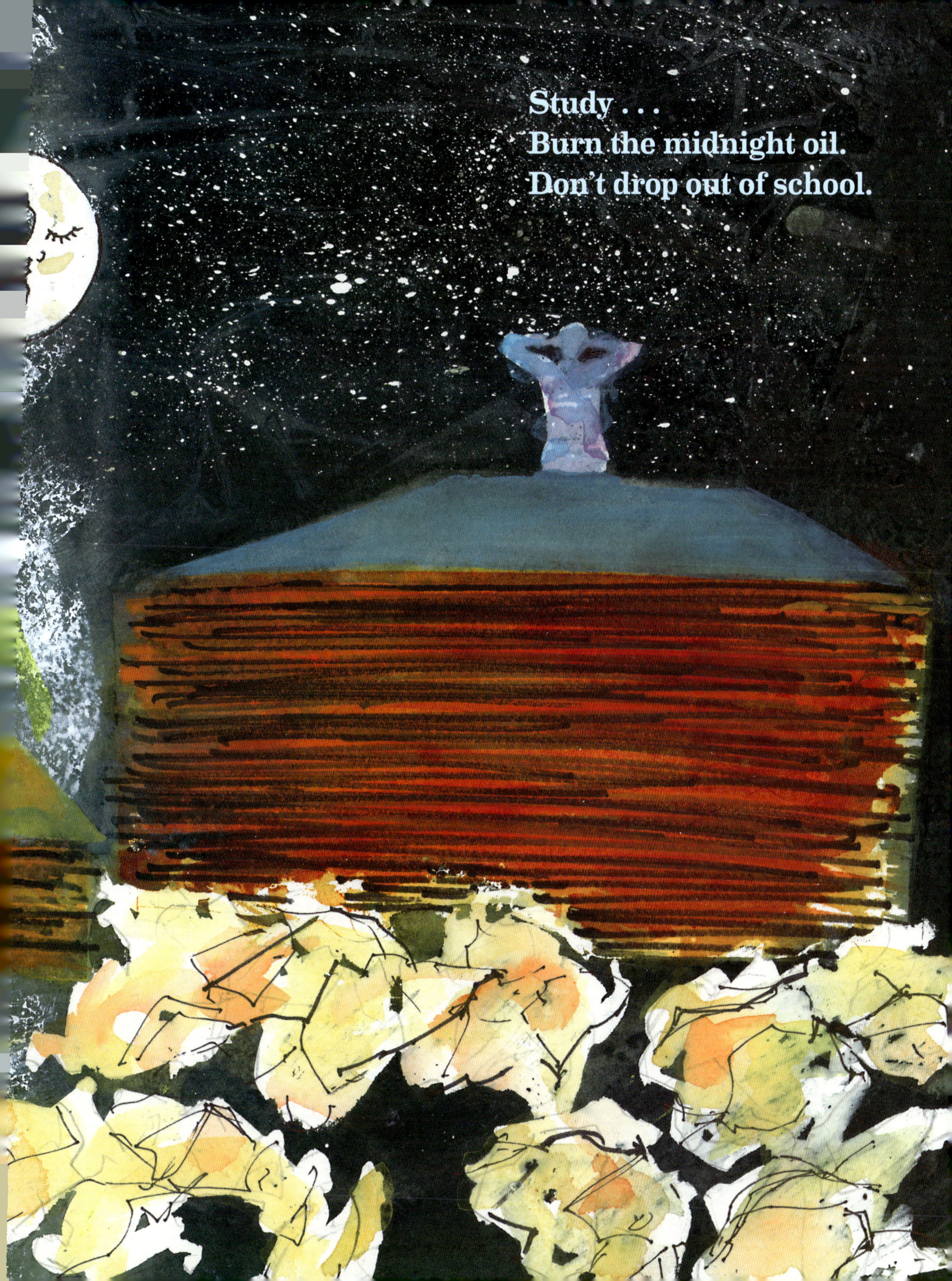

Study . . .
Burn the midnight oil.
Don't drop out of school.

LIVE . . .
DISCOVER . . .
DO A JOB WELL.

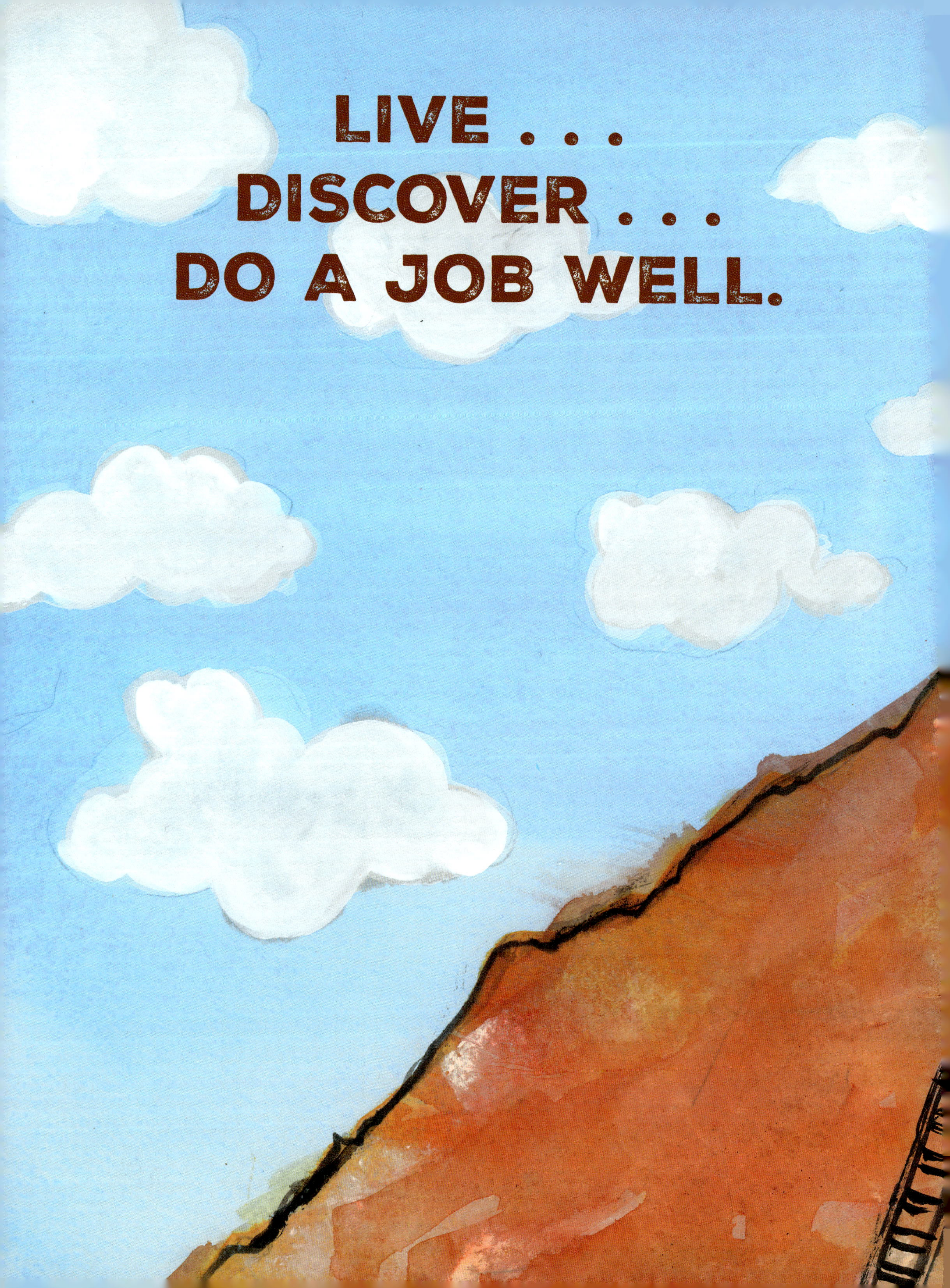

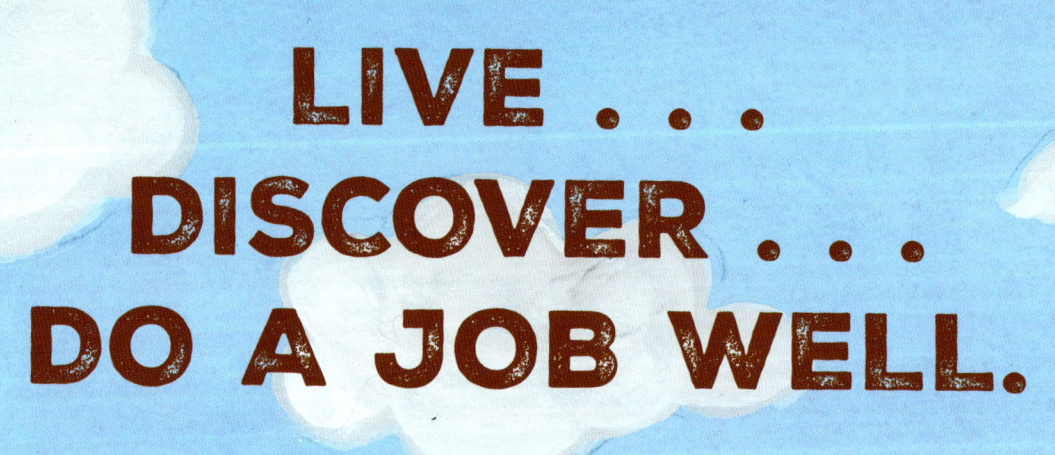

Like Michelangelo . . .
Beethoven, Leontyne Price . . .
Like Shakespeare . . .

BE THE BEST WHATEVER YOU ARE.

Noble Black men and women have
walked through long nights of oppression,
and they've risen up—blazing stars.

Booker T. Washington rose up!
Marian Anderson rose up!
Roland Hayes rose up!

George Washington Carver (science star) reached up
to shine with scintillating beauty.

Then came Jackie Robinson . . .
Willie Mays . . . Jesse Owens . . . Joe Louis . . .
and Muhammad Ali with the conviction of the poet,
Black affection, and soul.

FINALLY—your life's blueprint must be a commitment to beauty, love, and justice.

DON'T HATE.

DON'T LOSE YOUR SELF-RESPECT.

SEEK TO MAKE YOUR NATION BETTER.

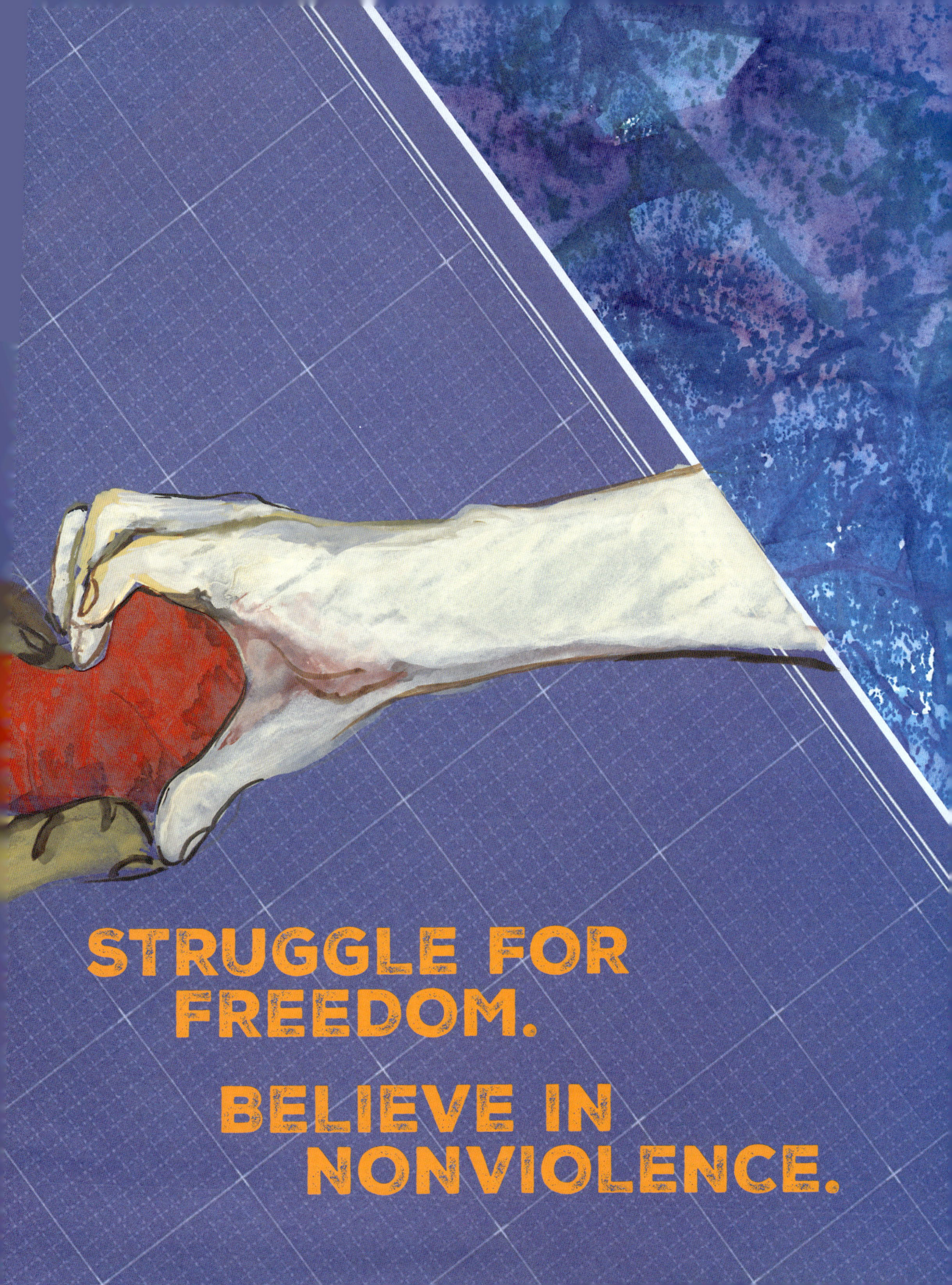

Young people . . .
We have won significant victories
with a method that does not destroy life or property.
Our slogan must not be "Burn, baby, burn."

It must be . . . **BUILD**. . .
ORGANIZE. . .
LEARN . . . so we can earn.

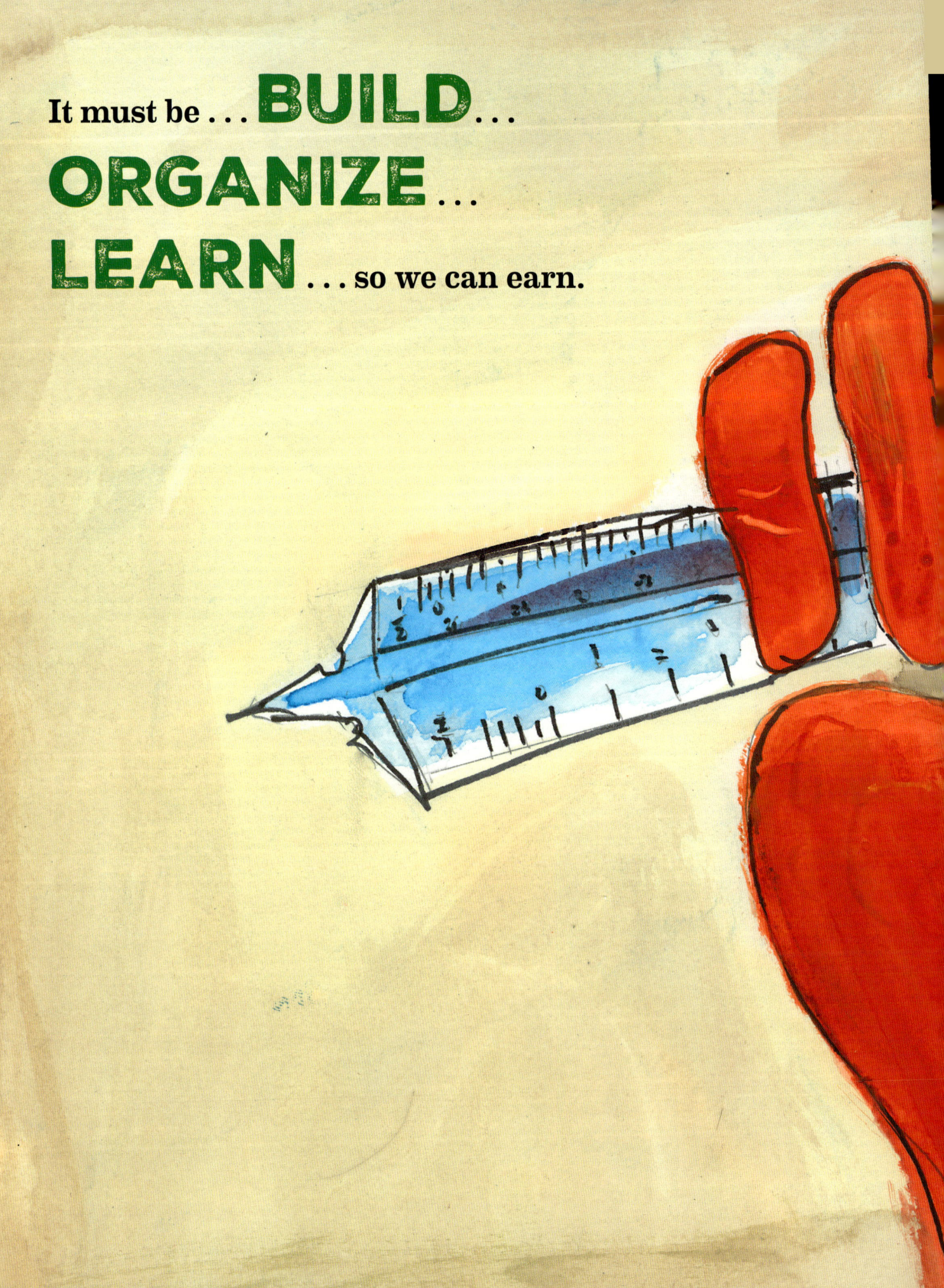

Transform injustice into justice.

Dream . . . **DREAM!**

Let nobody stop us.

Langston Hughes wrote,
Life ain't no crystal stair.
It's . . . tacks, boards torn up,
places with no carpet—bare.

BUT, DON'T STOP!

WHAT IS YOUR LIFE'S BLUEPRINT?
HISTORY BEHIND THE SPEECH

The day was October 26, 1967, in Philadelphia, Pennsylvania. While preparing for a freedom rally at the city's Spectrum arena, Dr. Martin Luther King Jr. took time to visit Barratt Junior High School where he asked students, "What is your life's blueprint?"

As a Nobel Peace Prize recipient, Dr. King posed this question to ignite the students' dreams, inspire their determination, and initiate their sense of duty to democracy. Spoken in his measured and booming rhythms, Dr. King's twenty-minute speech was recorded that day and it is widely available online for your viewing. While "What Is Your Life's Blueprint?" was reduced to 277 words in my erasure poem, the complete text of the speech comprised of 1,765 words is also published and widely available in Dr. King's many books of collected speeches.

When you locate the complete speech for independent reading or viewing, you will discover that Dr. King's message remains urgent and relevant. Here in the twenty-first century, to achieve personal success and collective peace, each of us must plan for a bright future, celebrate our unique identity, pursue every endeavor with excellence, resist hatred, and keep marching onward to engage life with a heart full of hope, determination, and grace. Dr. King's blueprint for a good life in his day remains the foundation for a shining life today.

To see a video of Dr. King delivering the speech, visit youtube.com/watch?v=ZmtOGXreTOU.

Barratt Junior High School students Theresa Palmer, Bernard Barnes, and Ethel Pierce talk with Counselor Louise A. Boxdale, next to a photo of Dr. King and a quotation from his speech, 1971.

HISTORICAL FIGURES MENTIONED IN THE SPEECH

Michelangelo (1475–1564) Italian sculptor and painter

William Shakespeare (1564–1616) English playwright, poet, and actor

Ludwig van Beethoven (1770–1827) German composer and pianist

Booker T. Washington (1856–1915) Black Virginian and founder of Tuskegee University

George Washington Carver (1864–1943) Black scientist and inventor born in Missouri

Roland Hayes (1887–1977) Black composer and lyric tenor born in Georgia

Marian Anderson (1897–1993) Black opera singer and activist from South Philadelphia

Langston Hughes (1901–1967) Black Harlem Renaissance poet and playwright from Missouri

Jesse Owens (1913–1980) Black Alabama sprinter who won four Olympic Gold Medals in 1936

Joe Louis (1914–1981) Black Alabama boxer and heavyweight champion from 1937–1949

Jackie Robinson (1919–1972) Georgian, first Black to integrate Major League Baseball in 1947

Leontyne Price (1927–) Black Metropolitan Opera star from the piney woods of Mississippi

Willie Mays (1931–2024) Black Major League baseball star from Alabama

Muhammad Ali (1942–2016) Black Olympian and heavyweight boxing champion from Kentucky

WRITE YOUR OWN ERASURE POEM

Erasure poems are a form of found poetry, where the words are drawn directly from a longer existing text like a newspaper article, novel, or speech. Using ink, paint, pencil, or correction fluid, the poet erases various words in their original order to either enhance the source's meaning, create a contradiction, or add a humorous, nonsensical effect. Keep in mind that the power of poetry is its ability to express meaning in few words and erasure poetry amplifies this power. Let's get started.

1. Pick a portion of a newspaper or magazine article, speech, or novel.
2. Scan the portions and print four or five copies for this poetry activity.
3. Read your selected material many times to determine the message you want to express.
4. Using ink, paint, or correction fluid, erase various words to form your poem.
5. Make sure to erase at least 50 percent of the selected text.
6. Edit and refine your erasure poem on spare copies of the text.
7. Decorate your final poem with illustrations or collage.
8. Share your poem with others.

VICTORIES FROM THE AMERICAN CIVIL RIGHTS MOVEMENT (1956–1965)

Dr. King and activists in the Civil Rights Movement practiced nonviolence, using boycotts, marches, and sit-ins to dismantle injustice. Their efforts inspired three major civil rights victories. First, the yearlong Montgomery bus boycott of 1955 helped to integrate America's city transportation. Second, the 1963 March on Washington, with 250,000 participants, helped to outlaw segregation in public spaces with the signing of the 1964 Civil Rights Act. And finally, children, college students, and adults crossed Selma's Edmund Pettus Bridge in 1965. These six hundred activists inspired the Voting Rights Act of 1965, which outlawed voter suppression and intimidation.

Nonviolent resistance was part of Dr. King's blueprint for a rewarding life. As injustice and inequality continue to tear at the fabric of democracy, nonviolent resistance remains a popular strategy in social movements today.

A view of the crowd at the March on Washington for Jobs and Freedom on August 28, 1963.

BIBLIOGRAPHY

Aregood, Rich. "King Urges Militant Nonviolence Here." *Philadelphia Daily News*, October 27, 1967.

Cowper, William. "The Negro's Complaint." Schomburg Center for Research in Black Culture, Photographs and Prints Division, The New York Public Library. digitalcollections.nypl.org/items/510d47db-c530-a3d9-e040-e00a18064a99.

Hughes, Langston. "Mother to Son." In *The Collected Works of Langston Hughes*, vol. 1, edited by Arnold Rampersad. Columbia: University of Missouri Press, 2001.

King, Martin Luther, Jr. "What Is Your Life's Blueprint?" In *The Radical King*, edited by Cornel West, 65–70. Boston: Beacon Press, 2016.

Martin Luther King Jr. Center for Nonviolent Social Change. "MLK: What Is Your Life's Blueprint." YouTube. Recorded October 26, 1967. Video, 20:38. youtube.com/watch?v=kmsAxX84cjQ.

Washington, Kevin (former Barratt Junior High School student who attended Dr. King's speech). Telephone interview with the author, January 23, 2021.

Watts, Isaac. "True Greatness." bartleby.com/40/271.html.

Williams, Greg (son of Tony Williams, the teacher who introduced Dr. King before his Barratt Junior High School speech). Telephone interview with the author, July 5, 2021.

ACKNOWLEDGMENTS

I want to thank Kevin Washington for speaking with me during my process of composing this poem. Kevin was a Barratt student on October 26, 1967. He was in the auditorium the morning Dr. King gave his "Blueprint" speech. Hearing details of that historical moment offered me a palpable inspiration that moved me to finish my final draft. I am forever grateful.

TEXT PERMISSION

PICTURE CREDITS

To Julian Alexander Barnes, architect and dreamer —*AFD*

Dedicated to our children,
who are the future of our society —*EBL*

Calkins Creek
An imprint of Astra Books for Young Readers,
a division of Astra Publishing House
astrapublishinghouse.com

Printed in China

ISBN: 978-1-6626-8031-1 (hc)
ISBN: 978-1-6626-8032-8 (eBook)
Library of Congress Control Number: 2025935673

First edition

10 9 8 7 6 5 4 3 2 1

Design by Barbara Grzeslo
The text is set in Eames Century Modern.
The illustrations are done in mix medium, watercolor, markers, color tissue, and gouache.